WILDLIFE IN BLOOM SERIES

Little Hedgehog

BY AUTHOR & CONSERVATIONIST

LINDA BLACKMOOR

ISBN: 978-1-966417-22-4 (PRINT)

PUBLISHED BY QUILL PRESS. LINDA BLACKMOOR'S TITLES MAY BE PURCHASED IN BULK FOR EDUCATIONAL, BUSINESS, FUNDRAISING, OR SALES PROMOTIONAL USE. FOR INFORMATION, PLEASE EMAIL HELLO@LINDABLACKMOOR.COM

FIRST PRINT EDITION: 2025

LINDA BLACKMOOR
WWW.LINDABLACKMOOR.COM

SPECIES

Hedgehogs are small, spiny mammals in the Erinaceidae family, with around 17 different species found in parts of Europe, Asia, and Africa. They belong to the same order as shrews, though their spines make them look very different. Most wild hedgehogs prefer woodlands, grasslands, or gardens where they can find insects and hide from predators. Breeds, like the African pygmy hedgehog, are popular as pets.

SPINES

A hedgehog's back is covered with up to 7,000 spines, each made of keratin, the same protein in human hair and nails. These spines are not poisonous but serve as a protective barrier when the hedgehog curls up. Young hedgehogs are born with soft, white spines that harden within days. As they grow, they shed these baby spines in a process called quilling, replacing them with adult spines.

DIET

Hedgehogs are generally insectivores, feeding on insects, worms, snails, and slugs. They also eat fruits, vegetables, and even small reptiles or amphibians when available. Their strong sense of smell helps them locate hidden prey in the soil or under leaves. In gardens, they are valued for keeping insect and slug populations under control.

HABITAT

Wild hedgehogs prefer temperate and tropical regions, seeking habitats with plenty of ground cover. They build nests in thick bushes, under logs, or within leaf litter to hide from predators and harsh weather. Urban gardens can also make good homes if there is shelter and a steady supply of insects. Adaptability in choosing their living spaces helps hedgehogs survive in changing environments.

NIGHT

Most hedgehogs are nocturnal, meaning they come out at night to hunt and explore. Their large eyes help them see in low light, while excellent hearing and smell guide them through the dark. During daylight, they usually rest in their nests or hideouts to avoid daytime predators. This night-focused lifestyle helps them avoid competition and remain hidden.

DEFENSE

When threatened, hedgehogs curl into a ball, tightening muscles that pull their spiny back into a protective shield. This reaction hides their vulnerable faces and bellies, making it hard for predators like foxes or owls to bite. They can remain curled up for a surprising amount of time, waiting for danger to pass. Sharp spines and a solid ball shape often discourage even determined attackers.

SENSES

Hedgehogs have a keen sense of smell and good hearing, crucial for finding food in darkness. Their eyesight is weaker but helps them sense movement nearby. Sensitive whiskers on their snouts also aid in navigation and detection of objects. These combined senses allow them to locate small prey and maneuver through tight spaces.

HIBERNATE

In colder climates, hedgehogs enter hibernation, slowing their heartbeat and body temperature to conserve energy. They look for safe spots like leaf piles or burrows, where they nest until spring. Before hibernation, they eat heavily to build up fat reserves that keep them alive through winter. This survival strategy lets them cope with times when food is scarce.

BABIES

Female hedgehogs give birth in summer, with litters of 4 to 7 hoglets that are born blind and soft-spined. Mothers nurse them for about four to six weeks, after which they start venturing out to learn how to forage. During this time, the hoglets develop stronger spines and open their eyes. By around two months old, they can begin living on their own.

VOCALS

Though often solitary, hedgehogs use squeaks, grunts, and snuffles to communicate. They also rely on scent marking to signal territory or identify each other. During mating season, males circle and sniff females, sometimes making huffing noises. Subtle body language, like raising spines slightly, can signal annoyance or defense readiness.

SALIVA

A unique behavior in hedgehogs is self-anointing, where they produce foamy saliva and spread it on their spines. They do this after encountering strong smells, like certain plants or chemicals. Scientists suggest it might help mask their own scent or provide a mild deterrent with new odors. Though not fully understood, self-anointing is one of the most intriguing hedgehog habits.

LIFESPAN

In the wild, hedgehogs typically live 2 to 4 years, facing threats like predators, car accidents, and habitat loss. In captivity, where they have fewer dangers and a steady diet, some can reach 5 to 7 years or more. Health issues like obesity or dental problems can shorten their lives if not cared for properly. Regular checkups and a balanced diet are crucial for pet hedgehogs.

HEDGEHOG FACTS #13

ADAPT

Hedgehogs thrive in different climates thanks to their flexible diet and ability to protect themselves. Some species tolerate desert conditions with minimal water, while others do well in rainy woodlands. Their spines and curling defense let them coexist with varied predators across continents. This adaptability has helped hedgehogs remain widespread despite human development.